/

HIGH EXPOSURE

Los Angeles Times

Book Development Manager/Editor: Carla Lazzareschi
Copy Editor: Pat Connell
Design: Mary Peterson

ISBN 1-883792-51-7
Copyright © Los Angeles Times 1999
Published by the Los Angeles Times
Times Mirror Square

First printing February 1999

Printed in the U.S.A.

HIGH EXPOSURE

Hollywood Lives | found photos from the archives of the *Los Angeles Times*

Amanda Parsons

Los Angeles Times

Los Angeles, California

FIG. 3

IF THE NOTION OF MODERN-DAY CELEBRITY HAS A FLASH POINT, SURELY IT MUST BE LOS ANGELES.

When the movie business moved west to this outpost of sunny skies, a motley alliance of studio publicists, star wannabes and journalists invented the illusion of Hollywood, a magical place where fortunes and careers could be made—or squandered— in the pop of a flashbulb. This Hollywood gave the world new standards for both glamour and the value of publicity.

It was here in Hollywood that the concept of "the star" was born and, with it, the assumption that we—the public, the fans—have an absolute right to the most intimate details of our favorite star's everyday life. In much the same way that dime novelists turned dusty cowboys into champions of the American frontier and sportswriters turned baseball players into role models for a nation, journalists, and their attendant photographers, turned actors in the new celluloid medium into the heroes of the entertainment age. In the process, these celebrity stories sold not only newspapers, but movie tickets. The beat set in the 1920s continues to this day. Every new face in Hollywood is made to feel that it needs publicity to succeed. They get this attention when they want it— and when they do not. And the fame they seek brings an attendant high exposure that is not always a pretty picture.

While this is an old and oft-repeated story today, at the dawn of Hollywood the clamor for celebrity attention was new and barely tested. Celebrity had not yet turned a shy English Princess Di into a hounded media product whose death may or may not have been a direct result of media pursuit. Celebrity had not yet turned the president of the United States into a tabloid king, his family and lovers into media fodder. Indeed, it is mind-boggling to consider that the very notion of Hollywood celebrity began when Mary Pickford was innocently crowned "America's sweetheart."

As the exploding media of entertainment and information technologies converged to create the first mass-market media superstars, the actors and actresses pictured here became as familiar as those in our family photo albums. The reason these pictures are so compelling is precisely because the stories behind then are so well known to us, so personal to our lives. We feel we know these people because we—right along with the subjects—have lived through so many of the stories that these photographs illustrate.

With the luxury of time, today we can see these photographs as something other than remnants of yesterday's news. They are more than reminders of history. They are social artifacts of a time when no one knew the consequences of fame. They are evidence of a time when few understood the public vulnerability and commitment that being a star required, fewer still the way being a celebrity shapes a personal-

FIG. 1

FIG. 2

FIG. 4

FIG. 5

FIG. 6

ity. In these exposures from Hollywood's past, we see the roots of our world-wide obsession with the famous.

For the *Los Angeles Times* and the *Los Angeles Mirror*, the newspapers of record for early Hollywood, the classic stars were not only icons, gods and goddesses; they were the stuff of daily, local news. It was a unique relationship. By mutual consent, the city's newspapers had almost unlimited access to the human beings whose real-life adventures and peccadilloes defined forever our popular image of Hollywood lives. The newspapers, the stars and the studios—sometimes working in tandem, as often working at odds—had the power to titillate and the power to shock. The power to create celebrity, the power to ruin it.

When Rudolph Valentino's (**FIG. 1**) bigamy was revealed, *Times* photographers were there to capture his image. We see him in this book, an actor without makeup, without flowing costumes, a man in a jam. When John Huston (**FIG. 2**), then known as "Walter Huston's son," had to defend against possible vehicular manslaughter charges, later dismissed, the *Times* photo captured his youth and his apprehension, his tie slightly askew, his too-short sleeves exposing his bony wrists and the tension in his hands. The newspaper was on the scene when trumped-up legal charges hounded Charlie Chaplin out of the country, and again when he returned in bittersweet triumph to get his honorary Oscar. The daily paper pictured charming rake Errol Flynn (**FIG. 3**) being acquitted of statutory rape as fans continued to seek his autograph, being hauled back into the police station for drunken brawling a few years later, and finally again at Union Station when he was returned to Los Angeles in a stark pine box for his funeral at age 50—dead in bed with his latest 17-year-old "protégée" attending him.

A fresh crop of actors and actresses arrived daily, then as now, bent on doing whatever it takes to make it in Hollywood, each following a singular path to the elusive inner sanctum. The photos emerge from the newspaper archives as if in a time warp: Marilyn Monroe, fresh-faced and eager to re-create herself. Jane Russell (**FIG. 4**), the local beauty queen. Clark Gable (**FIG. 5**), the rough, hunky roustabout. Being seen was part of the deal. Being put on parade was expected. Studios churned out publicity stills. Stars engaged in publicity stunts.

The daily grind of the presses shuffled the photos and stories in and out like flotsam and jetsam. The public loved seeing stars looking like stars. Marlene Dietrich (**FIG. 6**), who perhaps understood and controlled this dictum better that most, could literally kiss up to the reporter or create the illusion of sophisticated glamour on a moment's

FIG. 7

FIG. 8

FIG. 9

notice. By contrast, Greta Garbo created her distinct appeal by running from the press, a precedent that no one else has carried off so well.

Sometimes the exposure seems harmless, even charming. Did Virginia Mayo (**FIG. 7**) really lose her swimsuit in the nasty surf, or were Sal Mineo's clothes really torn off by a giggling group of girls? Has there ever been a more beautiful accident victim than Audrey Hepburn (**FIG. 8**)? Or a cuter appendectomy patient than Burt Lancaster? A more perfect family man than Jimmy Stewart? Have a couple in love ever glowed more than Clark Gable and Carole Lombard? Or continued to delight in each other as much as Paul Newman and Joanne Woodward? We sigh with awe and envy.

But there is a decidedly dark side to this exposure. The camera finds Sir Laurence Olivier, the king of actors, on the edge of tears, removing his sedated manic wife Vivien Leigh from her Hollywood psychiatrist, transporting her out of Hollywood back to England, where he will eventually divorce her and she will die young of the ravages of mental illness and tuberculosis. Robert Wagner sneaks back to wife Natalie Wood's coffin for a last intimate good-bye. The long lens catches it, and the world rights to the *Times* photo are sold to a public eager to touch his sorrow. Mae West (**FIG. 9**), whose professional life was spent exposing sexual hypocrisy, is last seen in this book as a parody of herself, dedicating her own exaggerated image in wax. After her death, her home is ransacked by souvenir hunters. How much ownership do we the public feel we deserve?

Is the price of celebrity too high? Can the loss of privacy ever be controlled? Judy Garland pictured at barely 12 is a little girl with the remnants of a cold sore. But she was a little girl whose life never belonged to her alone. The cover photo is a still life of exposed ambiguity. As she artfully creates the high arch of her brow in the mask of her makeup, the ubiquitous cameraman waits his turn in the shadows. I take a magnifier to the print. The cigarettes are there, the bars on the window to the outside, the tissue box. No pills. I get lost in her eyes, her hands, the purse of her lips. How many generations will be pulled into the complexity of this talented and tragic child of Hollywood? The picture tells it as no words can express.

Frank Sinatra (**FIG. 10**) is seen signing autographs on a ladder stenciled "Grip Dept." We don't have to see his face to know him. The camera eats him up. His charisma shines like a torch. A later photo shows him in court, arrested for assaulting a news photographer. The news shot looks like a scene from a movie. The charge is dismissed, but for much of his career his photos take on a surly, defensive quality.

A sincere Dorothy Dandridge (**FIG. 11**) and an overly prim Maureen

FIG. 10

FIG. 11

FIG. 12

O'Hara fight back in court against unscrupulous media that go far beyond reporting to fabricating news. A public that cannot get enough is fed by a cottage industry of pseudo-reporters and photographers who stretch reality.

To discover these photos is to realize how much these icons impact us. The photo of Frances Farmer (**FIG. 12**) being incarcerated and sent for psychiatric evaluation and, as we now know, an eventual lobotomy, penetrates the conscience, especially when viewed in the context of her young, brilliant, eager self, photographed at LAX on the cusp of stardom never quite achieved. What role did her celebrity play in her downfall?

Elizabeth Taylor's (**FIG. 13**) life emerges as a full public peep show. Her private grief at husband Michael Todd's death penetrates like a bullet from the photograph of her, looking small and stricken, returning from his services. But there, in the closed window of her limousine, is a reflection of an unknown fan staring—the public scrutiny she can, and will, never escape.

The tense 1953 photo of Desi Arnaz (**FIG. 14**) and Lucille Ball in a backyard press conference denying communist leanings records a grim spectacle, our Lucy being forced to denounce her youthful ties to her grandfather, whose political leanings were clearly to the left, and her early voter registration as a Communist. Hollywood's stars were under siege for their politics. The taint of any communist association sent a current of terror through the creative juices of Hollywood. The only thing red about her, she claimed, was her hair—and it was fake. She, at least, passed the "red quiz." For scores of others, careers, fortunes and reputations were ruined.

Yet six years later, at the height of the Cold War, when Soviet premier Nikita Khrushchev, visited the U.S., he took his family, an entourage of American politicians and assorted secret service agents to watch Frank Sinatra croon on the movie set of *Can Can*. Here was the political descendant of Lenin and Stalin ogling and clapping like the rest of us fools. And here was Hollywood pandering to him with government encouragement—as if Senator Joseph McCarthy and his House Un-American Activities Committee had never existed.

To each photograph, both photographer and subject bring their own reality. And, with the perspective of time, we observers bring our own interpretations. The camera catches an aging Veronica Lake (**FIG. 15**) trying to make a comeback. Her early press releases claimed she wanted to be a doctor. But a face like an angel and an unruly lock of hair made her a Hollywood goddess. Kim Bassinger won an Oscar for impersonating a Lake impersonator in the 1997 movie *L.A. Confidential*. But by the time that movie was supposed to have taken place, in the late 1950s, the real Veronica Lake's luxurious estate had long since been taken over by the IRS. She disappeared in the night to a marginal street life and occasional jobs slinging hash in roadside coffee shops.

FIG. 13

When the *Times* photographer found her, 20 years after her ignominious departure, she was back at Paramount Studios in Hollywood, stooped and dying, trying to recapture the glamour lost, still signing autographs for her ever less glamorous fans, rhinestone sunglasses covering what the eyes had seen, a zippered polyester pantsuit replacing the silks and lace of her glory years. Is the scene portrayed overwhelmingly sad? Or does it give hope to us all that the allure can be resurrected, if only for the brief click of the camera's shutter?

FIG. 14

And what of Marilyn Monroe? The camera and we fans clearly love her more than she loved herself. When she chose to remove herself from the world, it was in a room stripped of any of the style we would expect from the most revered of screen goddesses. The paint on her bedroom walls is peeling. Cheap satin sheets and fringed pillows remain on the bed where her body was removed. Old newspapers and shopping bags litter the floor.

FIG. 15

When photo researcher Gayanna Raszkiewicz and I found the lost negative of her deathbed scene in a file drawer, we held it to the light and thought the folds left in the bedding still held her lifeless body. When the print came back, the ghosts in the picture were even more haunting, the reflection of the news photographer off the window to her bedroom, the pills used to take her own life haloed by the reflection of the camera's flash.

If, as has been speculated, the celebrity death is the dramatic conclusion of the celebrity life, Marilyn's death is a paradigm for a Hollywood that creates its stars and spits them out. Here was a pristine artifact of that death, lost for decades, painful to see. No detectives. No maids. Just a lonely room with a photographer there to record the last glimpse of her high exposure.

MOVING IN

Circa **1950** | digital scan from original print

"Underexposed," says the *Los Angeles Mirror* caption as **MARILYN MONROE** returns to Hollywood to rebuild her career after several movieland starts and stops, some success in New York as a model, and a nude calendar photo that reportedly earns hundreds of thousands of dollars for the publisher and just $50 for her. She is not to remain in the shadows for long, however. Soon she will reinvent herself as the most famous sexy blonde ever to grace the movie screen. As if to help that quest along, the newsroom uses photo paint to highlight and enhance her breasts in the original photo, which is pulled from the file to run in 1952 as her career is beginning to take off.

December 7, **1937**

Irish actress **GREER GARSON** arrives in Hollywood with her MGM contract in hand. Rumor has is that she has the style and talent to succeed the retiring Greta Garbo and Norma Shearer as the screen's reigning monarch. The elegant redhead's first film, *Goodbye, Mr. Chips*, will earn her an Academy Award nomination.

4

December 31, **1947**

Accomplished stage actress **PATRICIA NEAL** arrives In Los Angeles to film *John Loves Mary*. She will then star opposite leading man and eventual lover Gary Cooper in *The Fountainhead*.

February 12, **1937**

On a prerelease publicity tour for their film *Personal Property*, **JEAN HARLOW** returns to town from Washington, D.C. with co-star **ROBERT TAYLOR**. Five months later, during the filming of *Saratoga*, the 26-year-old thrice married platinum blond superstar, who proudly eschews underwear, will die of a mysterious infection in fiancé William Powell's arms.

6

September 7, **1935** | silver nitrate negative

On the edge of stardom, hoofer **FRED ASTAIRE** arrives at the train station with his luggage. Just two years before, he was given a small part opposite Joan Crawford in *Dancing Lady* despite the verdict from his screen test: "Can't act. Slightly bald. Can dance a little."

July 11, **1956**

Popular new star **KIM NOVAK** steps off the train upon her return to Los Angeles from a trip to the Cannes Film Festival.

July 30, **1957**

Stepping onto the tarmac at Los Angeles International Airport, Italian movie star **SOPHIA LOREN** claims envy because her archrival Gina Lollobrigida is the mother of a new son. But only months later, it is Loren who is being hyped by producer and soon-to-be-husband Carlo Ponti as the new Italian movie sex goddess.

November 3, **1936** | silver nitrate negative

Carrying a Russian literature text under her arm, former University of Washington honor student **FRANCES FARMER** is marked for greatness as she disembarks in Los Angeles after her first screen endeavor.

November 6, **1936** | silver nitrate negative

Starlet **CAROLE LOMBARD** appears in court to officially add the "e" on the end of her newly created screen name. Studio mavens apparently thought the moniker "Jane Peters" not catchy enough for the movie marquee.

May 18, **1939**

JANE RUSSELL, second from left, makes her debut as "Miss Van Nuys" in the San Fernando Valley Queen Contest. From this taste of acclaim, she will study with famed acting coach Max Reinhardt before producer Howard Hughes anoints her the reigning queen of voluptuousness in a nation-wide chest hunt for the lead in *The Outlaw*.

Circa Mid-**1920**s | glass negative

Members of the latest ensemble of child actors to star in Hal Roach's **OUR GANG** series of comedy shorts hold their contracts. Assembled more for their physical characteristics than their acting experience, the changing groups of little performers and their mischievous antics began entertaining audiences in 1922, when the first troupe spun off the *Sunshine Sammy* comedies. In 1955, nearly 100 of the original skits will be packaged for television as *The Little Rascals*, the same title used for a 1994 feature film revival.

August 14, **1935** | silver nitrate negative

July 18, **1947**

LEFT: The man she is later to call "the *real* Wizard of Oz," Louis B. Mayer himself, auditions **JUDY GARLAND**, age 11, and without a screen test signs "the little girl with the great big voice" to MGM. Already a veteran of the vaudeville stage as part of the "Gumm Sisters Kiddie Act," the former Frances Gumm will co-star in a "swing vs. the classics" musical short subject, *Every Sunday*.

RIGHT: Director Irving Pichel first used five-year-old **NATALIE WOOD** as an extra in a movie shot in her hometown of Santa Rosa, California. He remembers her three years later at age eight and signs her for a feature film, *The Bride Wore Boots*. Her next movie will be the Christmas classic *Miracle on 34th Street*.

14

Circa **1930** | silver nitrate negative

Circa **1935** | silver nitrate negative

LEFT: Emotive **JACKIE COOPER**, an alum of *Our Gang*, is nominated for a Best Actor Academy Award at age nine for *Skippy*, a tearjerker directed by his Uncle Norman Taurog.

RIGHT: Chubby-cheeked **JANE WITHERS**, age 10, one of the top-ranking child stars, shows off her latest contract. By age 13, her popularity suffers as the ingenue parts go to prettier peers. Rare character parts will keep her semiemployed until a series of long-running television commercials puts her boundless vitality back before audiences in the person of Josephine the Plumber.

June 13, **1945**

Singing and dancing phenomenon **SHIRLEY TEMPLE** was an Oscar winner at age 10 and almost a has-been by age 12. By the time she receives her high school diploma from Westlake School, her cute, saucy style films which brightened the Depression have been replaced by the more serious themed ones of the World War II era. She is doing so little acting at this point that she no longer needs her on-set tutors and receives her schooling on campus with her peers.

16

April 17, **1939**

"Gal Swimmer," says the lensman's note on this photograph of 15-year-old champion aquanaut **ESTHER WILLIAMS**. She is giving swimming lessons to the children of Hollywood while she awaits a chance to dive into acting.

Circa **1925** | glass negative

His father took him to Oklahoma to drill for oil, but his first wife, actress Josephine Dillon, brought aspiring actor **CLARK GABLE** to Hollywood. Fourteen years his senior, she coached him in speech and movement, and, shortly after this glamour pose was shot, she will treat him to false teeth to compensate for a bad front tooth cap.

Circa **1927** | silver nitrate negative

Comely **MAE WEST** moves her sex-symbol reputation from the New York stage to the movies. By innuendo, double entendre and self-parody, she is trying to stay one step ahead of the Hollywood censors.

October 15, **1945**

When you are a star, glamour can be anyplace the photographer shoots. **WILLIAM POWELL** takes his debonair *Thin Man* looks to the back room of the Los Angeles Courthouse. Is the black stocking a joke or an accident? As was done with most photographs of the era, the photographer clearly planned to "art" out extraneous background with some of the photo department's amply applied supply of white touch-up paint.

20

November 13, **1940**

Leading lady **CAROLE LANDIS** shows off "the best legs in town" as she poses for photographers in the press room of the courthouse where she is appearing for her second divorce. A woman "ahead of her time," according to actor-friend and possible lover Rex Harrison, she will appear in nearly 30 films including some of her own productions.

December 28, **1937**

One of the most dependable leading ladies in Hollywood is **BARBARA STANWYCK**, who followed her first husband, vaudeville headliner Frank Fay, to Hollywood. She is now in the courthouse signing her own contracts.

December 31, **1935** | silver nitrate negative

In Hollywood on a Paramount contract, actress **IDA LUPINO** and her father, film comedian **STANLEY LUPINO**, descend from a British theatrical family dating back to the 17th century. Ida was discovered when her mother, actress Connie Emerald, auditioned for a part. The casting agent chose her teenage daughter instead.

February 10, **1951**

GRETA GARBO signs papers that make the Swedish-born actress an American citizen—the only time she willingly allows a *Los Angeles Times* photographer to take her picture.

Circa **1925** | glass negative

Studio founder and Metro-Goldwyn-Mayer vice president **LOUIS B. MAYER**, center with wife Edith, waves hello to Hollywood—and waiting photographers—after a trip east by train. Daughters Irene and Edie, left, and others join the power-wielding mogul, the prime architect of the powerful studio system.

MEET THE PRESS

August 8, **1946**

"She was so happy to be back in Hollywood, she was willing to kiss anybody," reads the caption on this photo of **MARLENE DIETRICH** planting a big one on the cheek of *Los Angeles Times* reporter Clark Roberts. Entertaining American troops overseas and recording anti-Nazi broadcasts kept the stylish German actress out of town for much of World War II. Even for the calculatingly aloof Dietrich, the work of being a star demands an ongoing flirtation with the press.

June 27, **1944**

April 9, **1937** | silver nitrate negative

June 22, **1952**

YVONNE DE CARLO shows off the scrapbooks from her worldwide promotional tour. The necklace and flowing garments perhaps portend her later television career: cavorting with vampires as Morticia Addams in *The Munsters*, precursor to the big screen hits *The Addams Family* and *Addams Family Values*.

ABOVE LEFT: **MARGARET O'BRIEN**, already a star at age eight, delivers an autographed picture to *Los Angeles Times* reporter J. D. McAviney for a charity event.

BELOW LEFT: Being interviewed after her film debut with Judy Garland in *Every Sunday* is **DEANNA DURBIN**. Before opting for a wealthy retirement at age 26, she will become Hollywood's highest-paid female star.

February 24, **1958** | digital scan from original print

January 19, **1935** | glass negative

ABOVE: **CHARLES COBURN** relaxes in bed with a book as the *Los Angeles Times* reporter who followed him all day, Art Ryon, feigns exhaustion beside him at 4 a.m.

BELOW: Humorist **WILL ROGERS** consents to a career-enhancing interview while sitting atop his polo pony.

Syndicated newspaper columnist **HEDDA HOPPER**, who left acting to become a celebrity reporter on Hollywood stars, is crowned with another of her trademark collection of hats: this one from actor **JACKIE GLEASON**, television's bus driver Ralph Kramden in the popular series *The Honeymooners*.

July 7, **1949**　|　digital scan from original print

"Naughty wave pulls suit off **VIRGINIA MAYO**, left," reads the headline. The accompanying article describes a wild situation: a one-piece swimsuit that disappeared about 25 feet from shore, a friend who happened to be there with "an extravagantly long, thick, bath towel," and a waiting photographer who sent the above snap to the *Times*. The next month she will be named "best undressed woman of the year" by the Colorado Sunbathing Society. Sheer serendipity or the work of a PR master?

32

Screen darling-of-the-moment **SAL MINEO**'s clothes also did a reported disappearing act, this time lost to a "giggling group of teenagers" who coincidentally were trailed by a *Los Angeles Times* photographer. Still costumed in an Indian headband, Mineo tells a smirking policeman that he'd "rather wear a barrel than have a fan accused of stealing."

August 15, **1943**

FRANK SINATRA retreats to the highest point around—the Grip Department's ladder on the RKO studio lot—to sign autographs as fans push for a personalized memento.

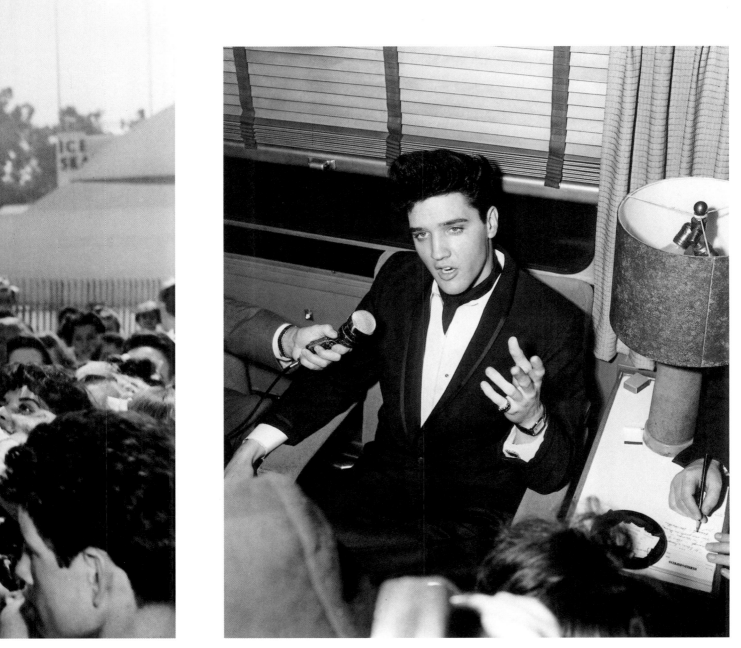

May 18, **1957**

Discharged from a European stint in the Army, singing, gyrating love magnet **ELVIS PRESLEY** announces
his intention to return to stardom and to restore his half-grown military-trimmed hair to its previous
pompadoured splendor.

October 27, **1954**

News photographs beg the question: How much is contrived and how much is real? What is public and what is private? **MARILYN MONROE** sits primly beside attorney-to-the-stars Jerry Giesler during her 10-minute divorce hearing from baseball great Joe DiMaggio. But is her tongue a reaction to the incoming tide of reporters or is she merely moistening her lipstick?

August 10, **1949**

"Smiling happily, **JIMMY STEWART** and his new bride leave the church after the wedding ceremony," says the photographer's note on this print. "Photographer foreground," he adds "is goddam MGM man, the s.o.b."

March 11, **1937**

Once bankrolled by Joseph Kennedy, aging actress and fashionable show-woman **GLORIA SWANSON**, attempts to revive her film career in Hollywood. She even submits to a humiliating screen test, but the part does not materialize. Thirteen years later at age 52, in a screen imitation of life, she will make one of the profession's most memorable comebacks in the role of *Sunset Boulevard*'s Norma Desmond, reportedly first offered to then-57-year-old Mae West, who claimed she was much too young for the role.

Golden Globe Best Actor **MARLON BRANDO** is toasted by presenter **MAUREEN O'HARA** after winning for his role in *On the Waterfront*. Brando's Best Actor performance will also prevail at the Academy Awards a few weeks later. In 1973, he will reject a Best Actor Oscar in a protest against the treatment of Native Americans.

October 2, **1949**

The idealized frontier hero who doesn't drink, smoke or swear transcends filmdom to become a symbol of America. **WILLIAM BOYD**, who effectively became Hopalong Cassidy when he acquired all rights to the character and learned to ride his horse Topper, greets his young look-alike fans.

April 13, **1956**

SAL MINEO signs autographs as his date, actress **GIGI PERREAU**, waits at the premiere of her film, *The Man in the Grey Flannel Suit*, at Grauman's Chinese Theater.

March 23, **1945**

ROY ROGERS, the singing "King of the Cowboys," signs an autograph for a young fan, Virginia Weibel, 11, at the induction station where the western movie hero, the victor over scores of silver-screen villains, took his Army physical. More than 2,000 Roy Rogers Fan Clubs dot America as World War II draws to a close.

Star **JOAN CRAWFORD**, in velvet cape, autographs larger-than-life picture for her fan club at the Warner Brothers Theater premiere of *Torch Song*.

April 19, **1966**

WARREN BEATTY's embrace of sister **SHIRLEY MACLAINE** temporarily separates them from the pop of the flashbulbs and the crush of the crowd eager to see the stars follow the path to the inner sanctum of the Oscar ceremony.

March 22, **1956**

Bespectacled and befurred Hearst newspaper gossip writer **LOUELLA PARSONS** notes details for her Oscar Awards column. **NATALIE WOOD**, nominated for her supporting role in *Rebel Without a Cause*, pauses with her date, **TAB HUNTER**. Wood lost to Jo Van Fleet in *East of Eden*.

June 27, **1957**

Commemorating their movie hit *Gentlemen Prefer Blondes* in the favored Hollywood way, **MARILYN MONROE**, left, and **JANE RUSSELL** plant their hands in a slab of freshly poured cement in front of Grauman's Chinese Theater on Hollywood Boulevard.

October 25, **1939**

MICKEY ROONEY watches *Babes In Arms* co-star **JUDY GARLAND** push her palm into the cement as her high-heeled sandals await a similar immersion into enduring fame near Rooney's right foot.

April 20, **1957** | digital scan from original print

SHELLEY WINTERS pushes fiance **ANTHONY FRANCIOSA** in the face to keep him quiet as the actor is bound in handcuffs at the police station for attacking a news photographer who tried to take the couple's picture. After a trial, Franciosa will be taken in shackles to spend 10 days in jail for assault.

April 10, **1947**

Arrested on battery charges for slugging New York columnist Lee Mortimer, **FRANK SINATRA**, his career in a lull, appears in Beverly Hills municipal court in full view of his glaring accuser. Although the complaint is dismissed, with reports of a $25,000 out-of-court settlement, Sinatra's relationship with the news media is forever soured.

September 4, **1957**

Confidential magazine, which makes Hollywood gossip its stock and trade, doesn't escape the wrath and attorneys of its celebrity subjects. In one case, actress **DOROTHY DANDRIDGE** denies under oath the magazine's contention of an "outdoor tryst" on a Lake Tahoe singing engagement.

August 3, **1957**

In her suit against *Confidential* magazine, **MAUREEN O'HARA** swears that she could not have been at a "petting party" that became "the hottest show in town" when she "cuddled in Row 35" of Grauman's Chinese Theater. Her proof? A passport showing that she was in Europe at the time of the alleged incident.

February 26, **1941**

Cloaked in solitude, **GRETA GARBO** maintains her cultlike image as she runs from the camera—yet again.

March 23, **1956**

Signature purse in hand, flags of the soon-to-be-united countries in the background, **GRACE KELLY** waves good-bye to a successful, Oscar-winning movie career and a horde of newsmen and well-wishers as she boards the plane that will take her from Los Angeles to her wedding to Prince Rainier III, of the House of Grimaldi, the ruler of Monaco. Forever after, she will be "Princess Grace," a true Royal.

January 5, **1944**

She danced before Britain's royal family at age three and teamed with *Our Gang*'s "Alfalfa" (Carl Switzer) at age 10. At age 11, this promising child actress, **ELIZABETH TAYLOR**, is signing a contract with MGM that will give her not only her first starring role, in *National Velvet*, but will tie her to that studio until the early 1960s.

May 6, **1950** | digital scan from original print

Ever fascinating **ELIZABETH TAYLOR** and husband, **CONRAD NICHOLSON HILTON, JR.**, leave for their media-hounded honeymoon after a storybook wedding that was keenly exploited by MGM to promote the 17-year-old Taylor's latest picture, *Father of the Bride*.

March 28, **1957**

ELIZABETH TAYLOR and her third husband, producer and showman **MICHAEL TODD**, react after he receives an Oscar for Best Picture for *Around the World in 80 Days*.

57

March 26, **1958**

ELIZABETH TAYLOR kisses her diamond ring as she returns to Los Angeles from the Illinois services for husband, Michael Todd, killed in an airplane crash. Her brother Howard is beside her, and others move to protect her as her limousine readies to depart from the airport. The image of an unknown bystander is reflected in the vehicle's window.

April 19, **1961**

The morning after the Academy Awards ceremony, **ELIZABETH TAYLOR** and fourth husband, crooner **EDDIE FISHER**, celebrate her Best Actress Oscar for *Butterfield 8*.

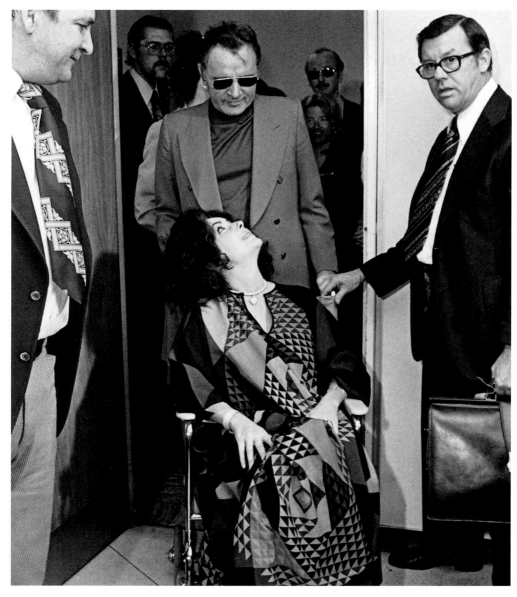

December 10, **1973**

An ailing **ELIZABETH TAYLOR** gazes fondly at her husband, British actor **RICHARD BURTON**, as he wheels her to their plane at Los Angeles airport en route to Italy for a reconciliation of their on-again, off-again marriage. Burton blamed relentless media attention for turning what he expected to be a passing affair into an international *cause célèbre*, a roller-coaster ride of passionate romance, marriage and breakups.

April 25, **1986**

MICHAEL JACKSON, a singing sensation since his childhood, and friend **ELIZABETH TAYLOR**, who has survived a similar celebrity path, enjoy opening day at the horse races at Hollywood Park.

BEING SEEN

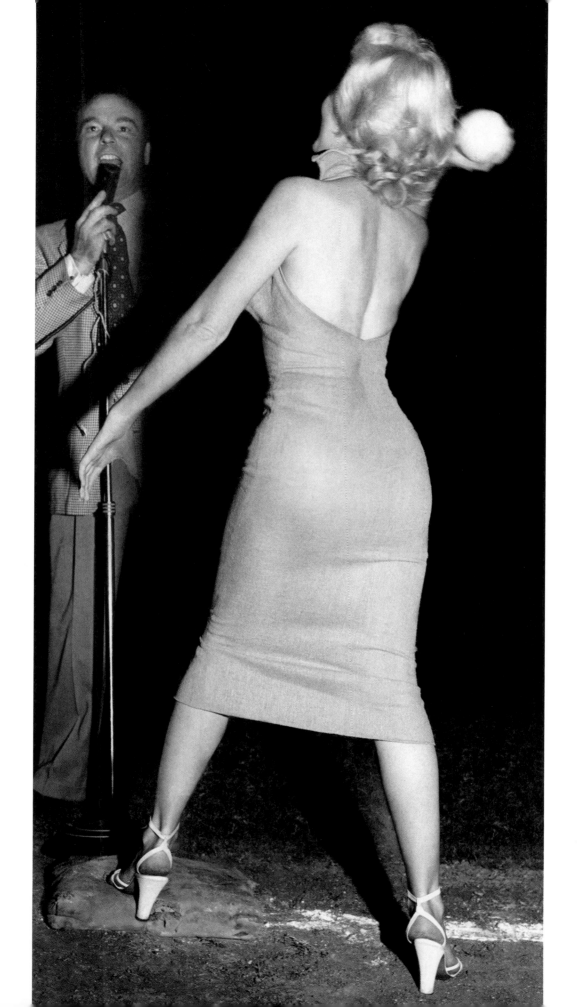

March 26, **1940**

Arguably the film industry's most romantic couple, **CAROLE LOMBARD** and **CLARK GABLE** spend a day at Hollywood Park, cheering the horses and socializing with the regular crowd of celebrity race fans who attend every weekend.

Circa **1952** | digital scan from original print

PREVIOUS PAGE: **MARILYN MONROE** shows off her signature curve as she tosses a baseball past the announcer at a charity ball game.

December 28, **1939** | silver nitrate negative

Busby Berkeley musical comedy star **RUBY KEELER**, recently separated from superstar husband Al Jolson, putts.

November 3, **1947**

February 26, **1948**

ABOVE: **JACK BENNY**, left, and **BOB HOPE** are deep in predinner conversation as fellow movie industry party goers peep at the famous profiles. Hope is being feted by the Friars Club.

BELOW: Studio head **LOUIS B. MAYER**, right, congratulates comedian **JIMMY DURANTE** on being awarded the Friars Club's Heart of Gold Award.

January 28, **1950**

Comedian **ED WYNN** takes the curtain as well as the award for Best Live show at the first presentation of television's equivalent of the Oscars, given by the Academy of Television Arts and Sciences. *The Ed Wynn Show* aired for only one year.

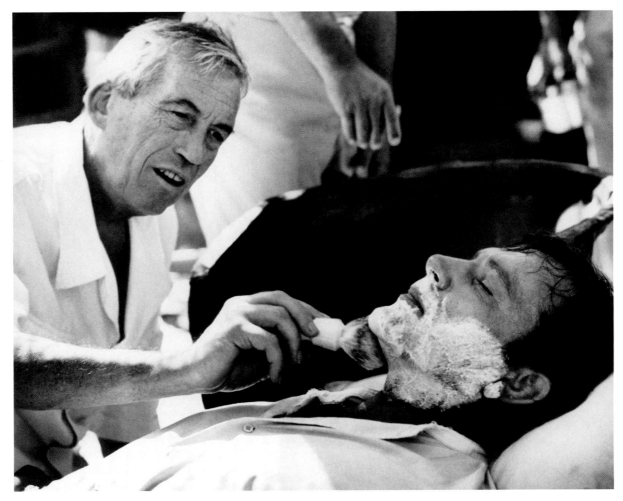

March 1, **1964** | digital scan from original print

Director **JOHN HUSTON** lathers up star **RICHARD BURTON** for a shave on set of *Night of the Iguana*, being shot in Puerto Vallarta, Mexico.

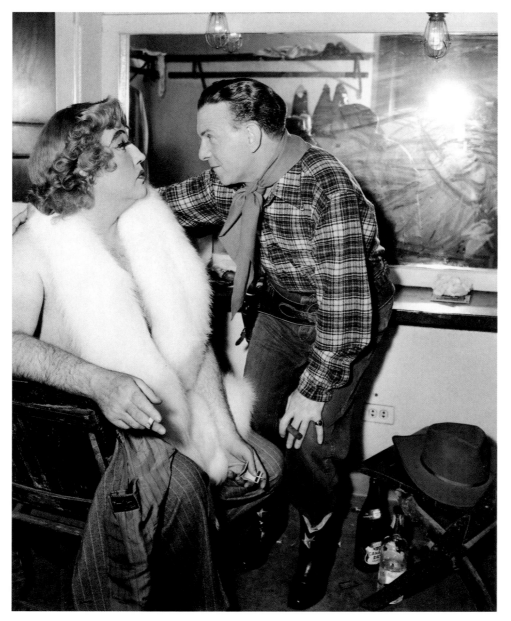

April 24, **1950**

With an all-male cast, Los Angeles' Friars Frolics has **BRODERICK CRAWFORD** in boa and makeup as a substitute for **GEORGE BURNS**' usual comedy partner, wife Gracie Allen.

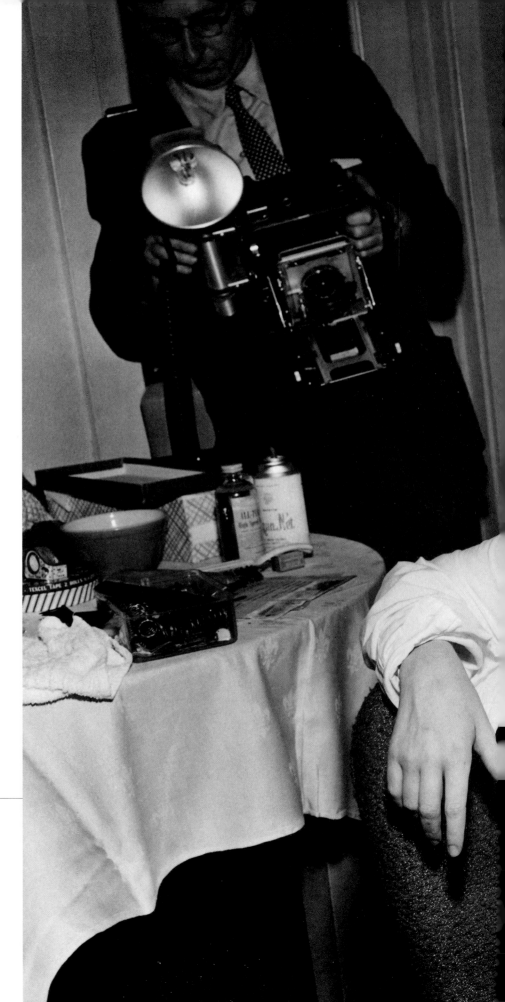

"Jubilant Judy," read the caption that accompanied a photo from this assignment when it ran in the *Los Angeles Times*. But this previously unpublished image of **JUDY GARLAND** preparing for a singing engagement at Los Angeles' Greek Theater seems to reflect a more ambiguous reality.

70

August 15, **1940**

Gone With the Wind Supporting Actress winner **HATTIE MCDANIEL** was not merely the first African American to win an Oscar, but the first to attend an Academy banquet as a guest rather than a waiter.

November 21, **1958**

Actress **TALLULAH BANKHEAD** is combing her curls for opening of play *Crazy October* when its author, **JAMES LEO HERLIHY,** drops in to wish her luck.

April 21, **1959**

Musical star **JUDY HOLLIDAY** clutches telegram of good wishes in her dressing room before the premiere of the Broadway hit *Bells Are Ringing* which will usher in the 22nd season of the Los Angeles Civic Light Opera Association—and move to the silver-screen the following year.

September 6, **1948** | digital scan from original print

She did not make it as a New York chorus girl, but **LUCILLE BALL** dons a showgirl headdress, Lucy Ricardo style, to play her part among other stars in what is billed as a "sawdust spectacle" for charity.

February 3, **1959**

AUDREY HEPBURN flashes a huge smile and gamely gestures "Okay" as an ambulance delivers her from Los Angeles airport to a local hospital. She was flown to L.A. after falling off a horse in Durango, Mexico, where filming of John Huston's *Unforgiven* screeched to a halt after the injury.

June 7, **1940**

Being seen around Hollywood in the latest convertibles is the thing to do. Here are the singing sensations **THE ANDREWS SISTERS**, La Verne, Maxine and Patty, on their way to the Southern California Music Fiesta.

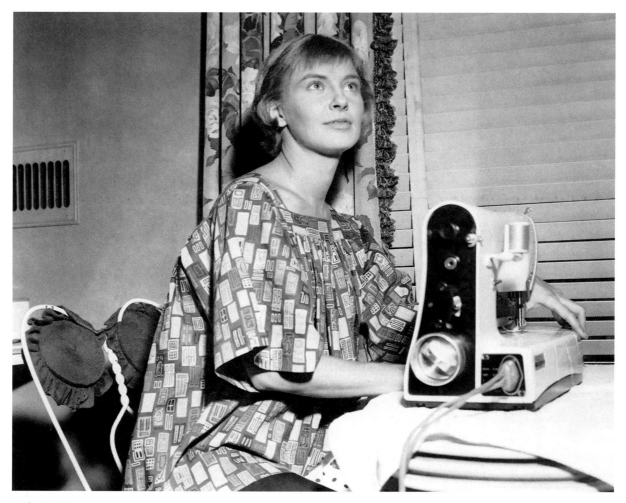

October 3, **1958**

Actress **JOANNE WOODWARD** sews as she awaits birth of first child with husband, actor Paul Newman.

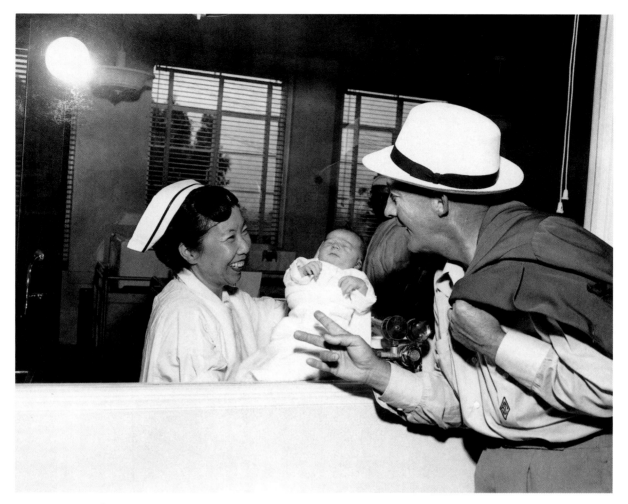

August 9, **1958**

BING CROSBY greets his new son, Harry Lillis Crosby III—"a neat eight pounds" when he leaves to go home—held by attendant Eva Huang in nursery at Queen of Angels Hospital.

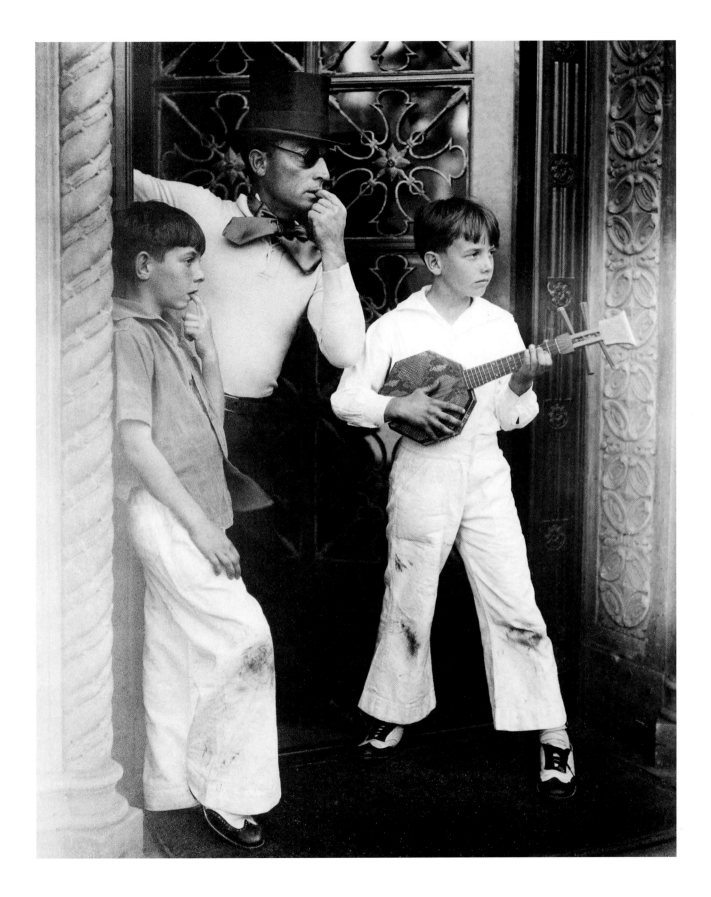

April 1, **1951**

JOAN CRAWFORD questions son Christopher Terry when the boy is brought home after a three-hour disappearing act because he was denied chocolate syrup. "Joan decreed a tanning," says the caption.

Circa **1929** | glass negative
LEFT: Ever unsmiling comic BUSTER KEATON, whose film world was crowded with willful machines, clowns around with real-life sons, Joseph ("Jimmy") and Robert. Their mother, Natalie Talmadge, is the sister of actresses Constance and Norma Talmadge.

June **1959**

Musical star **PAT BOONE** poses his family—Lindy, 3, wife Shirley, Cheryl, 4, Laurie, 1, and **DEBBIE**, 2—at the airport as he arrives to film science fiction flick *Journey to the Center of the Earth*.

April 19, **1955**

JIMMY STEWART, his wife, Gloria, twin daughters Judy and Kelly, and stepsons Michael and Ronald leave their Beverly Hills home for Easter Sunday services.

July 11, **1962**

JOANNE WOODWARD and husband **PAUL NEWMAN** converse at the funeral of producer Jerry Wald.

May 12, **1987** | digital scan from original print

A silver anniversary later, **JOANNE WOODWARD** and **PAUL NEWMAN** exchange glances as they work their way through the crowd at gala premiere of their film *The Glass Menagerie* at the Cannes Film Festival.

May 18, **1965**

PATRICIA NEAL, pregnant with her fifth child and recovering from a debilitating stroke, is helped from a hospital cart by her husband, popular children's writer **ROALD DAHL**. Partially paralyzed and with severely impaired speech, she will fight back courageously to win an Oscar nomination in 1968 for *The Subject Was Roses*. The couple will later split.

April 8, **1957**

Producer **DAVID O. SELZNICK** and actress **JENNIFER JONES** return to Los Angeles through the catacombs of the airport. Selznick groomed the brunette beauty for stardom, cast her in her first Academy award-winning role in *Song of Bernadette* and married her after her divorce from actor Robert Walker. Selznick's death left her financially ailing and suicidal. She later married mega-mogul Norton Simon.

January 18, **1948**

TYRONE POWER returns to his studio duties from the airport, where he reportedly waited in vain for "his latest romance" to appear, or so said the studio spin meisters.

November 15, **1951** | silver nitrate negative
PREVIOUS PAGE: Divorced from first wife Nancy two weeks before and remarried for just a week, **FRANK SINATRA** arrives at Los Angeles International Airport from honeymoon with wife **AVA GARDNER**, the earlier spouse of Mickey Rooney and then musician Artie Shaw.

After the funeral of husband Humphrey Bogart, actress **LAUREN BACALL** leaves All Saints Episcopal Church, Beverly Hills, with her daughter Leslie and mother Natalie Bacal Perske. Mourners crowded the street for a last memory of the superstar, who died at 57 of cancer of the esophagus.

May 13, **1962**

FRED MacMURRAY and wife **JUNE HAVER** carry in furniture as they move back into their Brentwood home, which was partly destroyed in the Bel-Air fire the previous November.

November 19, **1943**

Silent film superstar comedian **HAROLD LLOYD** stands elegant in the basement ruins of his house fire.

September 24, **1952**

Awaiting a remodel, **JAYNE MANSFIELD** and body builder husband **MICKEY HARGITAY** sit in lavish emptiness, his barbells occupying the hearth in the living room of their $78,000 home. It is soon to be treated to a $75,000 redecorating that will outfit it with a heart-shaped fireplace and fur-covered bathroom walls.

January 11, **1958**

A smitten nurse beams and temperatures rise as she administers some TLC to actor **BURT LANCASTER**, in the hospital for an emergency appendectomy.

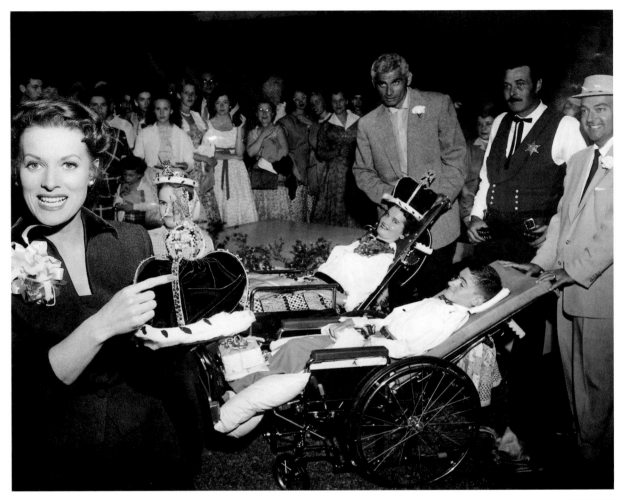

July 26, **1956**

MAUREEN O'HARA, left, **JEFF CHANDLER**, center, and Sheriff Lucky, center right, help present Mr. and Miss Breathless and Little Whisper crowns to polio victims at a Los Angeles polio center.

March 26, **1958**

JOHN WAYNE, **MAURICE CHEVALIER** and **ANTHONY QUINN**, left to right, share a laugh with producer **JERRY WALD**, far right, at rehearsals for Academy Awards. Quinn, nominated for *Wild Is the Wind*, lost out to Alec Guinness for *The Bridge on the River Kwai*.

February 7, **1955**

Without his usual partner, Charlie McCarthy, ventriloquist **EDGAR BERGEN** charms his wife Frances' stuffed snake at an elaborate costume party thrown by ice skating actress Sonja Henie. The event drew scores of revelers from the Hollywood film community. The rule: Come dressed as someone else.

July 3, **1940**

HEDY LAMARR shields her face from the gape of fellow actor **DON AMECHE**, while **JIMMY STEWART** awaits the action at Inglewood Racetrack. The stars came out to cheer the horses and support Red Cross Day.

May 20, **1959**

Suspense master **ALFRED HITCHCOCK** lets a rare grin escape as he and his wife, Alma, pause for fans and photographers on way to premiere.

June 29, **1956**

Actress **RITA MORENO** and friend, character actor **SAM GILMAN,** acknowledge fans as they follow the red carpet to the opening of *The King and I.*

December 27, **1960**

Fellow attendee ogles **TONY CURTIS** and wife **JANET LEIGH**—in celebrated $3,000 dress that she also apparently wore to Oscar ceremonies—on their way to opening of *Pepe*, in which she stars and he plays a cameo role.

November 5, **1930** | glass negative

In the third year of the awards set up by the Motion Picture Academy to honor its own, **NORMA SHEARER**, wife of MGM head of production Irving Thalberg, receives her Best Actress statuette for *The Divorcée*. "What do you expect?" said Joan Crawford of Shearer's win. "She sleeps with the boss." Academy president Cecil B. De Mille was away on vacation, but his telegram is read to the 650 in attendance: "Tell [the losers] that in a conflict between personality and ability it is impossible to say which will win."

March 1, **1940**

Gone With the Wind's much-ballyhooed Scarlett, **VIVIEN LEIGH**, holds her golden prize. She stopped Bette Davis' expected third win and, in a year of great films, brought to a record 10 the number carried home by the Civil War epic.

March 5, **1942**

GARY COOPER, Best Actor Oscar winner for *Sergeant York*, escorts **JOAN FONTAINE**, Best Actress for *Suspicion*, from the Biltmore Hotel banquet room as cameramen swarm. Rival and expected winner *Hold Back the Dawn*'s Olivia de Havilland prodded Fontaine, her real-life sister, to get up on stage, but their sibling animosity is heightened by this turn of events. de Havilland earlier confessed that despite pride in a profession that had honored her *Gone With the Wind* co-star and co-nominee Hattie McDaniel in 1940, she "had wandered out to the kitchen and cried" over that loss.

OLIVIA DE HAVILLAND finally wins one of those gold statuettes for herself, taking home the Best Actress prize for *To Each His Own*.

March 8, **1946**

Oscar askew, **JOAN CRAWFORD** busses **MICHAEL CURTIZ**, the director of her prize-winning best performance in *Mildred Pierce*. Although she was the first star to hire a press agent to mount a campaign for an Oscar, the actress claimed illness and did not attend the ceremony that evening. Nevertheless, a different staged photo of her bedside acceptance from the reportedly "gallant" Curtiz pushed all others off the front page the following morning.

April 19, **1961**

Producer-director-writer **BILLY WILDER**, who fled Nazi Germany with little money and no English, adds three more statues to his gold collection
when his film *The Apartment* brings him Oscars for Best Picture, Best Director and Best Writer.

April 6, **1965**

Actress **LORETTA YOUNG** rests her head on her arm and weeps as an emergency crew tries unsuccessfully to revive her longtime friend, business manager Jack Murton, who fell dead of a heart attack while appearing on her behalf in a Santa Monica courtroom. A *Los Angeles Times* photographer had been assigned to cover Young's court appearance in the contract dispute case.

December 3, **1981**

In a final farewell to his wife, actress Natalie Wood, actor **ROBERT WAGNER** kisses her coffin before leaving Westwood Memorial Park Cemetery after her funeral. Wood, who had admitted her terror of water in several press interviews, drowned when she fell from a dinghy in the waters off Southern California's Santa Catalina Island.

May 27, **1942**

Screen goddess **RITA HAYWORTH**'s mother, Volga Haworth Cansino, examines papers for court action on her daughter's divorce from husband Edward C. Judson. The former car salesman, 22 years her senior, plucked the performer from obscurity, guided her career, changed her name, had her hairline reshaped and transformed her from a Mexican dancer into an auburn-haired sophisticate. Divorce was his reward.

September 8, **1943**

Movie wunderkind **ORSON WELLES** embraces his bride, **RITA HAYWORTH**, after their surprise wedding ceremony in Santa Monica court. "I've got a secret," she told friends before the event.

November 11, **1947**

In knee-length mink coat, **RITA HAYWORTH** confers with her attorney and advisors just before her divorce from Orson Welles. "Mr. Welles showed no interest in establishing a home," she testified at the hearing. They have a daughter, Rebecca Welles, age three.

August 17, **1952**

RITA HAYWORTH and ex-husband **ALY KHAN**, whose marriage lasted a mere two years, turn to each other as they inform the press that their baby daughter, Princess Yasmin, suffered no ill effects from a near-fatal accidental ingestion of sleeping pills.

August 22, **1952**

A few days after the sleeping-pill scare, **RITA HAYWORTH** and **ALY KHAN** are caught by a photographer at a Los Angeles restaurant in what is described as a "farewell luncheon." Time clearly has run out on Hayworth's relationship with the jet-setter son of the Muslim spiritual leader.

STARS ON PARADE

August 27, **1942**

Each celebrity's call to colors during World War II is a triumph of studio publicity. But it hampers the effort to keep the home folks entertained without their favorite stars. Here, Lieutenant **RONALD REAGAN** shows up in uniform with wife **JANE WYMAN** for *Tales of Manhattan* premiere.

May 11, **1943**

ORSON WELLES was publicly hounded to enlist by the powerful Hearst newspapers, still angered by his production of *Citizen Kane*, clearly based on a thinly veiled portrayal of media mogul William Randolph Hearst. At his physical, he is classified 4-F, unfit for military service because of a variety of medical ailments.

JIMMY STEWART stands tall as he is inducted into the Army with other volunteers. By the end of the war he will be Colonel James Stewart, a bomber pilot who flew 20 missions over Germany.

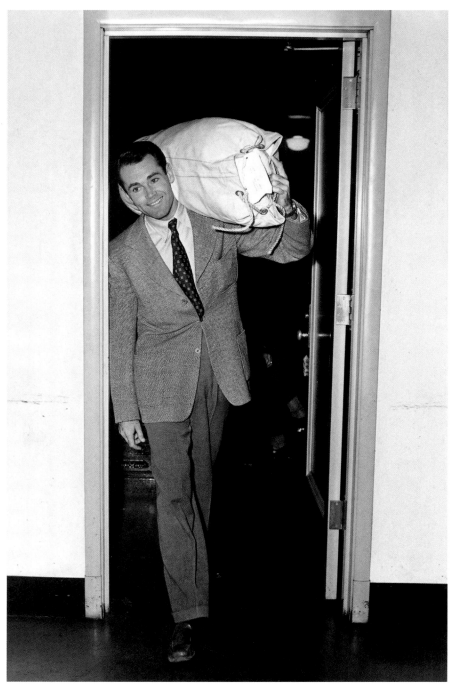

November 30, **1942**

HENRY FONDA is commissioned in the Navy and will win a Bronze Star and Presidential Citation for his service in the Pacific. But his service didn't begin until after producer Darryl F. Zanuck persuaded the War Department to first allow Fonda to finish a movie.

August 14, **1942**

His overwhelming grief at wife Carole Lombard's death in an airplane crash seven months before still shows in his eyes as **CLARK GABLE** enlists for combat as a private in the Army Air Force. Concern about him is such that that an MGM cameraman enlists at the same time and never leaves his side, which leads an officer to remark, "Gable is the only private in the history of the Army with his own orderly." Within two months he will be a lieutenant making training films.

August 14, **1942**

WALT DISNEY, right, whose studio was taken over by the Army, collects metal deer lawn ornaments for military scrap in his volunteer job with the war salvage chief, Joseph F. MacCaughtry.

January 31, **1938**

SHIRLEY TEMPLE, a mere nine years old but the top box-office attraction of 1938, cuts the cake at a party celebrating the 55th birthday of president Franklin D. Roosevelt. A trainload of Hollywood stars and moguls traveled from California to the nation's capital for the event.

April 12, **1945**

BETTY HUTTON and other aspiring starlets entertain troops at the Hollywood Canteen.

October 27, **1947**

December 24, **1952**

ABOVE: Film actors flying to Washington, D.C., to protest the manner in which House Un-American Activities Committee (HUAC) hearings are being conducted purchase their tickets from an agent at Los Angeles Airport. From left are: **DANNY KAYE** (partially hidden behind **JUNE HAVOC**), **MARSHA HUNT**, **HUMPHREY BOGART**, **LAUREN BACALL**, **EVELYN KEYES** and **PAUL HENREID**.

BELOW: Director **JOHN HUSTON**'s political views are greeted by protests on picket placards as he and his entourage arrive for premiere of his film *Moulin Rouge*.

September 13, **1953**

LUCILLE BALL and husband **DESI ARNAZ** hold a press conference in the backyard of their San Fernando Valley home to explain her testimony before the House Un-American Activities Committee. When questioned about her onetime membership in the Communist Party by committee members investigating the alleged infiltration of communists into American institutions, notably Hollywood, Ball satisfied her audience and passed her "red quiz."

128

September 20, **1959**

Soviet premier **NIKITA KHRUSHCHEV**, his family and a mix of American and Soviet political leaders show enthusiasm for **FRANK SINATRA**'s singing on a visit to the set of *Can-Can* during a stop in Los Angeles.

CAPTURED BY THE PRESS

September **1933** | silver nitrate negative

JOHN HUSTON, 26, son of actor Walter Huston, appears at the coroner's inquest into the vehicular death of Tosca Izabel Roulien. The victim's husband, Brazilian heartthrob Raul Roulien, stared at the floor, then shook and slumped forward in his heavy overcoat as witnesses described the beautiful 23-year-old's ill-fated attempt to cross Sunset Boulevard at Gardner in heavy traffic. Huston was not speeding, they said, and the traffic signal was simply flashing yellow when the woman "loomed in the path of the car." The writer, actor and aspiring director took her immediately to Hollywood Receiving Hospital, where she died. Huston was absolved of any responsibility for the incident, but never again would drive a car.

Circa **1922** | silver nitrate negative

RUDOLPH VALENTINO, in a rare picture without makeup and flowing costumes, appears at court after his arrest on bigamy charges. The Italian star, an international phenomenon who is said to send women into hysteria, married actress–set designer Natasha Rambova (born Winifred Shaunnessy) before his first, unconsummated marriage was dissolved. Both wives are rumored to be lesbians.

Circa **1930** | silver nitrate negative

RIGHT: Jailed in New York for her play *Sex* and up against censors again with *Drag*, **MAE WEST** defends herself in one of the many cases brought against her for obscenity. The buxom actress, once billed as "The Baby Vamp," was the first to introduce the "shimmy" to the stage and caused protests by appearing as a male impersonator.

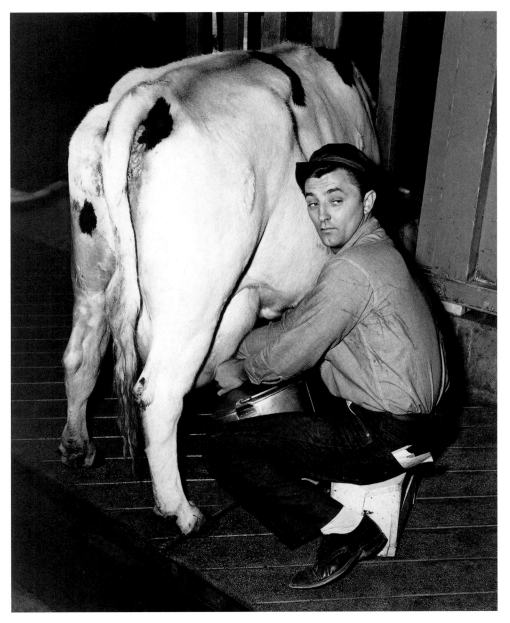

March 30, **1949**

Sentenced to a 50-day stay at Los Angeles County's Wayside Honor Farm after pleading guilty to marijuana possession, **ROBERT MITCHUM** shows off one of his newly discovered skills: milking ol' Bessie. The actor, who is already forming a "bad boy" reputation, took the plea-bargained sentence rather than face a public trial that could have ruined his career.

134

December 21, **1938** | silver nitrate negative

Radio funny man **GEORGE BURNS** returns to Los Angeles after being arrested on six counts and pleading guilty to two misdemeanors for trying to smuggle two jeweled bracelets into this country through New York customs. The judge was lenient because Burns was cooperative. Original photo editor aggressively scratched X's on negative, probably to mark nonessential people to be cropped from image when it appeared in the *Los Angeles Times*.

November 28, **1938**

MERLE OBERON shuffles court papers in a suit over a traffic accident that nearly killed her and brought a halt to the filming of Josef von Sternberg's spectacle *I, Claudius* with Charles Laughton. To her surprise, her chauffeur was found at fault.

July 6, **1936**

Widow and benefactor of Follies founder Florenz Ziegfield, renowned actress **BILLIE BURKE**, who will portray Glinda the good witch in the long anticipated *The Wizard of Oz*, defends herself in the so-called "stockings suit." Brought by a clothier to win payment for pajamas and stockings purchased a half dozen years before, the suit attempted to collect $558. Burke said that her late husband might have ordered the items, but she acknowledged receipt of only $40 worth of fancy hose and agreed to pay that. Municipal Judge Marchetti concurred.

November 18, **1937** | glass negative

CHICO, left, and **GROUCHO MARX**—without his painted-on mustache—wait in courthouse press room for legal action on their long-running federal case, the first prosecution brought for "borrowing" material from a previously rejected script. Followed closely in the press, the court's decision will assess each of the comedians the maximum possible $1,000 fine for the transgression. In addition, they will pay a $7,500 civil settlement.

March 4, **1936**

JAMES CAGNEY, left, discusses his contract suit with witness, actor **FREDRIC MARCH**. Acting dynamo Cagney is the first star to successfully challenge the binding studio contracts which allow actors little control over their roles and salaries. Both stars are accused of communist sympathies.

August 27, **1941**

DICK POWELL and wife **JOAN BLONDELL** enter court to testify as witnesses in what is called "the Hollywood swindle case." The couple deny knowledge of a "miraculous" cosmetic clay from Wyoming being touted by a local operator with whom they assert no connection. Claiming the supposed endorsement of a mythical "House of Blondell," accused swindler Dudley Abrams bilked Hollywood investors of $23,000 with his cosmetics company plans.

October 22, **1954**

CORNEL WILDE and wife, frequent co-star **JEAN WALLACE**, appear in court to be named guardians of her teenage sister.

December 15, **1954**

DANNY KAYE successfully denies an assault complaint brought against him. Reflecting his annoyance at the charges, he demonstrates how he merely defended himself against an attack by his accuser.

April 2, **1962**

JANET LEIGH tells a press conference of the black eye she received when knocked unconscious in a bathroom fall in her New York hotel. Concurrently, and without linking the events, she admits a separation from husband Tony Curtis. A divorce judge will later say her testimony "barely supported the charge of mental cruelty." She told newsmen Curtis "didn't want to be married any longer."

July 16, **1951**

Actress **MADGE MEREDITH** celebrates her 30th birthday with her release from Tehachapi Prison. Governor Earl Warren pardoned her after two and a half years behind bars because of evidence questions in her trial for kidnapping her business manager. She will return to television acting.

October 25, **1935** | silver nitrate negative

Undercover cop Harry Dean, left, impersonates **MAE WEST** in an attempt to capture an extortionist who threatened to throw acid in her face unless she delivered $1,000 to the corner of Sunset Boulevard and Bronson Avenue. After four nights of the ruse, however, West will play herself, allowing the police to finally capture the crook, a studio busboy.

December 11, **1964**

Kneeling on the floor of her Beverly Hills home, actress **CAROLL BAKER** holds a $75,000 diamond necklace that burglars overlooked when they took $11,000 worth of furs, recovered within the week.

EARTHA KITT, accompanied by fiance Bill McDonald, left, and police detective Chet Turner, visits a downtown pawnshop to recover items stolen from her home.

May 20, **1946**

HEDY LAMARR and actor husband **JOHN LODER** face down suspects accused of robbing their home. Breaking into tears, she sobbed that she felt sorry for the younger one. She will later be arrested twice for shoplifting and honored for her contribution to military communication technology.

October 30, **1941**

BASIL RATHBONE, famous for his movie portrayals of Sherlock Holmes, and his wife, Ouida Bergove, report a jewel robbery to the police.

February 1, **1966**

Three of **MICKEY ROONEY**'s four children with fifth wife Barbara Ann—from left, Kelly, 5, Kerry, 4, and Kyle, 3—are led from their Brentwood home by their mother's attorney, Harold Abeles. The children's mother, 29, was shot to death by her lover, actor Milos Milosevic, 24, with Rooney's gun before Milosevic took his own life. The act, 30 feet from the children's room, may have resulted from talk of a reconciliation. Rooney had filed for.divorce less than a week before, in a suit naming Milosevic. But the Rooneys had met earlier the day of the shooting and, press reports assert, may have had "a change of heart."

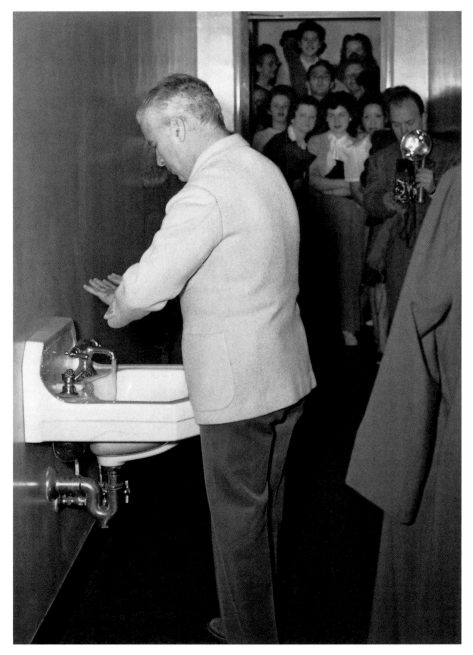

February 14, **1944**

CHARLIE CHAPLIN, perhaps the most talented film presence of the first half of the century, cannot even wash his hands without an audience—and photographers—as he goes on trial for violating the Mann Act, a rarely invoked law that makes it an offense to cross state lines for immoral purposes.

April 5, **1944**

After a dramatic trial in which the prosecution tried to establish that **CHARLIE CHAPLIN** provided money for his former lover to follow him to New York, the comedian-director holds hands with his lawyer, Jerry Giesler, front, as they anxiously await what will turn out to be a "not guilty" verdict.

December 28, **1944**

The photograph is manipulated, by the time-honored cut-and-paste method, but the blood test evidence presented by physician Dr. Newton Evans is irrefutable: **CHARLIE CHAPLIN** could not be the father of a child born to the woman Chaplin was accused of taking across state lines in an earlier case. Nevertheless, Chaplin, not represented by Jerry Giesler this time, loses the case and is ordered to pay child support. The legal scandal, along with trumped-up allegations of disloyalty, prompts U.S. immigration authorities to deny vacationing British citizen Chaplin a reentry visa. As a result, Chaplin will remain in self-imposed exile in Europe.

April 12, **1972**

Now with the British title of "**SIR**," **CHARLES SPENCER CHAPLIN** returns to Hollywood to accept an honorary Oscar for lifetime achievements, 28 years after leaving the United States.

154

July 29, **1946**

ERROL FLYNN welcomes his father, biologist Dr. T. Thomson Flynn, dean of the faculty of science at Queen's University, Belfast, Northern Ireland, at Los Angeles' Union Station. The elder Flynn will sail on an oceanographic expedition with the star of swashbuckling tales.

October 26, **1942**

On trial for two counts of statutory rape, **ERROL FLYNN** stops in the courthouse to sign an autograph for a fan. Attorney Jerry Giesler will encourage the jury's "not guilty" verdict by maintaining that the blade's reputation should have discouraged any respectable female from being alone with him on his yacht.

October 21, **1957**
RIGHT: In yet another example of **ERROL FLYNN**'s self-described "wicked, wicked ways," he is arrested and booked as a drunk after a fight at Hollywood's Screen Publicists' Ball. He nonchalantly reads the program from the event while awaiting bail posting.

October 21, **1957**

October 19, **1959**

ERROL FLYNN's body returns to L.A.'s Union Station in the traditional pine shipping box. Funeral services are being arranged for the star, who died in Seattle at age 50 in the company of his current 17-year-old girlfriend-protégée. Flynn's double and lifelong friend, Buster Wiles (in tie and hat), follows behind the coffin.

December 15, **1963**

FBI agents display $167,920 in cash, part of $240,000 ransom money recovered from the **FRANK SINATRA JR.** kidnapping. Sinatra Sr. was asked to deny under oath that the kidnapping was a publicity hoax. The perpetrators were convicted and jailed.

Shrouded in mystery, B-movie queen **MARIE McDONALD** is escorted from Indio Hospital near Palm Springs by British actor **MICHAEL WILDING** and a nurse after she was found wandering in the desert, the victim, she said, of a kidnapping. Later, the actress known as "The Body" broke down and admitted the story was an elaborate hoax, perhaps conceived to hype her sagging screen career.

July 30, **1925** | digital scan from original print

MARY PICKFORD demurely appears as a witness to help convict the men who conspired to kidnap her. Used as a decoy during the threat, the star drove around town in her glass-enclosed 1924 Rolls-Royce roadster with a sawed-off double-barrel shotgun at her side for protection. "We are the targets of all the nuts who come to Los Angeles," said her husband, Douglas Fairbanks Sr.

February 26, **1936** | digital scan from original print

Actress **VIRGINIA BRUCE** reads letter from kidnappers threatening to take her baby with ex-husband, star John Gilbert.

Circa **1930** | silver nitrate negative

Vivacious comedienne **THELMA TODD** poses with prop. The former teacher from Lawrence, Massachusetts, is a regular star for Hal Roach, who calls her "one of the most beloved actresses in the film plant." She co-starred in *Horsefeathers* with the Marx Brothers, and Groucho admitted his unrequited lust for her. Her own cafe in Malibu, which carries her name, is a mecca for the film colony.

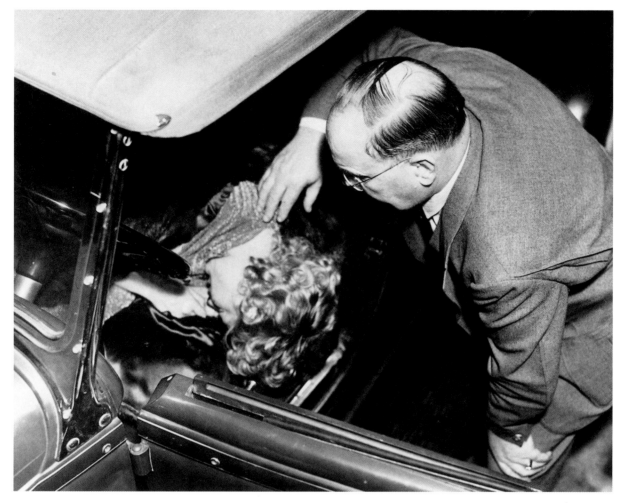

The bejeweled and fur-clad body of **THELMA TODD** is slumped in the car where she was found dead of asphyxiation in the garage of director Roland West. Was it an accident due to alcohol consumption, as determined by a coroner's inquest, or an unsolved murder connected to mysterious death threats and previous house break-ins? The question continues to baffle Hollywood sleuths.

December 17, **1941**

Matinee idol and theatrical scion **JOHN BARRYMORE** is interviewed at his baronial home, amid rumors that his lifestyle of excess is affecting his ability to get parts and remember lines.

April 9, **1943**

Comedian **W.C. FIELDS** is in and out of sanitoriums and in and out of court, including a protest of his doctor's $12,000 bill. Rosacea, the skin disorder from which he suffers, is popularly associated with alcoholism because of Fields' infamous addiction. In fact, while imbibing alcohol can worsen the facial condition, it is not the cause of the rash, pimples and bulbous red nose, all of which can be just as severe in a rosacea sufferer who does not drink at all.

April 26, **1950**

Friend Weston H. Eldridge, right, tries to keep a '40s leading man, Yale-educated **SONNY TUFTS**, from becoming a laughingstock after another embarrassing drunk-driving arrest. Tufts' drunken escapades and his habit of biting showgirls on the thigh are turning the mere mention of his name into a joke.

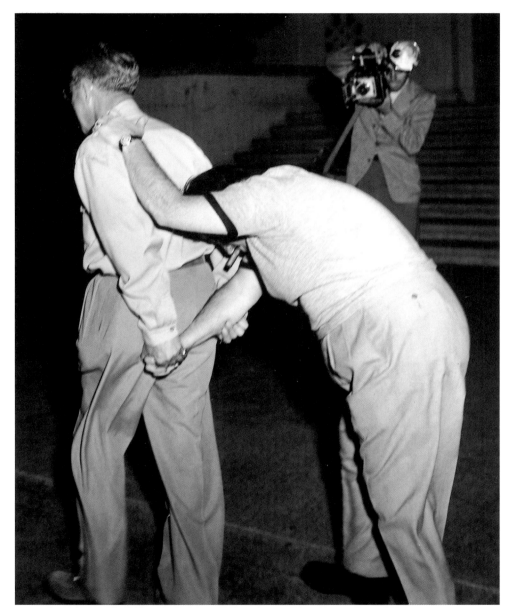

LOU COSTELLO, the pudgy half of the immensely popular, public-spirited Abbott and Costello comedy duo, ducks down to hide from the camera after his arrest for drunk driving.

February 3, **1944**

GAIL RUSSELL, the shy, talented actress signed to a film contract straight out of Santa Monica High School, will be linked in a romantic scandal with John Wayne.

July 5, **1957**

In the latest in a series of drunk-driving arrests, **GAIL RUSSELL** searches for her license after crashing her new convertible into a closed coffee shop at 8424 Beverly Boulevard, Los Angeles, and injuring the janitor. She will be found dead in her Hollywood apartment at age 36, surrounded by liquor bottles.

January 29, **1943**

FRANCES FARMER, once considered the brightest new star at Paramount, is again booked for drunk and disorderly conduct, a violation of her parole. This time she will be sent for psychiatric evaluation. Declared insane, she will spend most of the next decade in various mental institutions until she attempts a comeback in the late '50s.

November 9, **1950**

Already implicated in murders and gangland-style activities, the infamous "Mickey C," **MICKEY COHEN**, right, waits in court with his bodyguard, **JOHNNY STOMPANATO**, for the retrial of a Cohen henchman on felony gun possession charges.

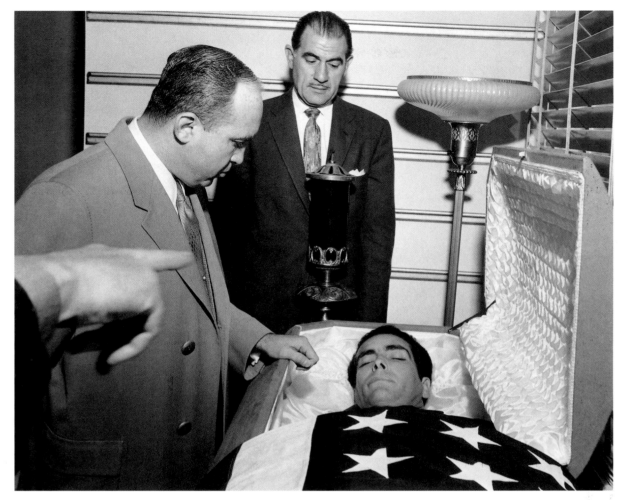

April 9, **1858**

MICKEY COHEN views flag-draped body of **JOHNNY STOMPANATO**, stabbed to death by Cheryl Crane, Lana Turner's 14-year-old daughter, who is being detained in juvenile hall pending charges of murder.

April 7, **1958**

LANA TURNER, lover of the late Johnny Stompanato, is helped into a waiting limousine by her chauffeur and attorney Jerry Giesler following a court hearing into charges that her young daughter murdered the mob bodyguard. Moments later [RIGHT], she is overcome by emotion inside the car as supporting arms reach out to comfort her. Eventually, daughter Cheryl Crane will be cleared of murder charges on grounds that she stabbed Stompanato in defense of her mother. But custody of Crane is temporarily taken from Turner and given to Turner's own mother.

April 9, **1958**

A pajama-clad **MICKEY COHEN** sits by the fireplace in his apartment and shares the contents of love letters written by Lana Turner to Johnny Stompanato to "prove" that the actress was really in love with his late bodyguard.

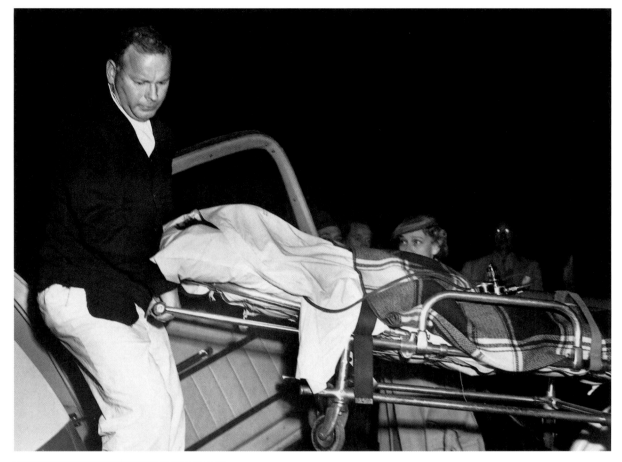

January 10, **1958**

A heavily sedated **VIVIEN LEIGH**, suffering yet another manic episode, is moved on a stretcher from an ambulance to a waiting plane that will take her home to England. Actor husband **LAURENCE OLIVIER**, below, supervises the transport, which is being made against the advice of her Los Angeles psychiatrist. Before getting on the plane, the anguished thespian sobbed in friend David Niven's arms. The illness of the Oscar-winning Leigh halted filming of *Elephant Walk* and eventually resulted in her being replaced in the film by Elizabeth Taylor.

As if in an elaborate stage set, actress **CAROLE LANDIS** lies lifeless on the bathroom floor, her head gently cradled on her jewelry box, her left hand holding a satin ribbon inscribed with the Lord's Prayer. A note to "Dearest Mommie" apologizes for the suicide by sleeping pills but says "there was no way to avoid it." Detectives searched for a motive. Although Landis had just left her fourth husband, speculation centered on a soured relationship with actor Rex Harrison, whom the wags dub "sexy Rexy."

181

April 27, **1955** | silver nitrate negative

Following in the wake of **SUSAN HAYWARD**'s nasty, months-long divorce and custody hearings with estranged husband Jess Barker, she is carried unconscious from her home and rushed to the hospital by police detectives alerted to a suicide concern by the actress' mother.

SUSAN HAYWARD and **DAVID NIVEN** congratulate each other on Oscar wins, he for *Separate Tables* and she for *I Want to Live!*

June 15, **1971**

SUSAN HAYWARD and husband, Jay Bernstine, attend annual Motion Picture and Television Relief Fund benefit at the Music Center in Los Angeles. This picture, reprinted after her death from a brain tumor, was used to describe her brave struggle with the disease. "Though seriously ill," the *Los Angeles Times* photo caption said, "[she] was one tough lady who made up her mind to go out this way."

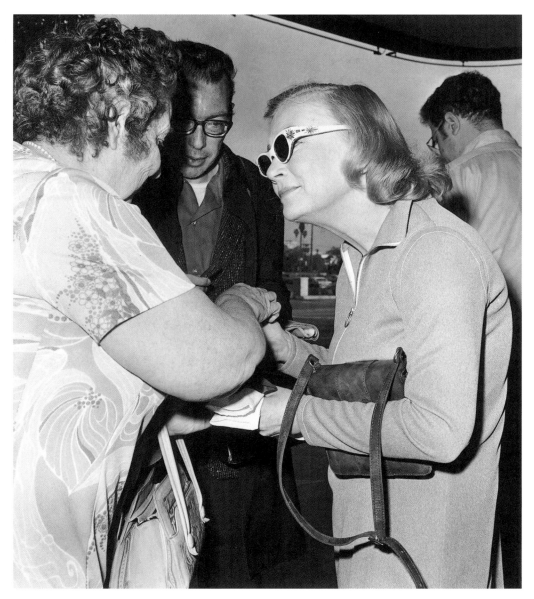

April 11, **1971**

Her intensity and style still intact, a ravaged **VERONICA LAKE** signs autographs at Paramount Studios. Twenty years before, after her 23-acre estate was seized by IRS agents, the sultry screen siren of the 1940s left Hollywood bankrupt. A newsman found her—enduring a life of menial employment, alcoholism and living on the streets—and encouraged her to pick up the pieces. Two years after this photo is taken, she will be dead at 53 from hepatitis.

December 19, **1972**

"Being a living legend is wonderful," says **MAE WEST**, center, "when you're living the kind of life I lead. Never a dull moment. Some dull men, maybe, but never a dull moment." The occasion was the unveiling of her likeness as "Diamond Lil," left, at the Movieland Wax Museum. At right is the real **GEORGE RAFT**, with whom she made her film debut in 1932's *Night After Night*.

August 6, **1962**

Deputy coroners remove remains of presumed suicide victim **MARILYN MONROE**, 36, covered by pale blue blanket.

August 6, **1962**

MARILYN MONROE's nude body was found at 3 a.m. on this bed in a bedroom of her cottage-style Brentwood home. The bedstand still holds an empty bottle that had contained about 50 Nembutal tablets, the probable fatal dose. Photographer's image and flash reflect off window.

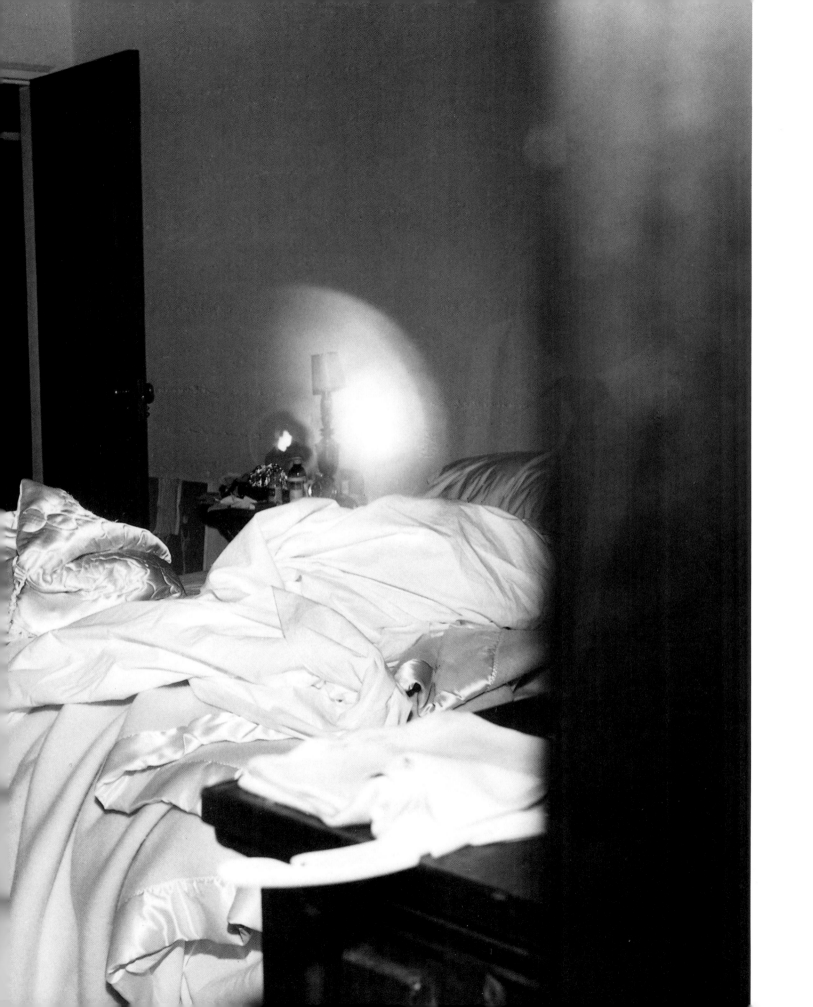

These extraordinary old Hollywood photographs come from the archives of two now-combined working newspapers, the *Los Angeles Times* and the *Los Angeles Mirror*. Since they were the ephemera of yesterday's news, there was no expectation that they ever would have aesthetic or historic value. Countless images were thoughtlessly destroyed or damaged beyond use. Nearly all photos and negatives dating before 1930 have simply disappeared. The existence of the discovered images chosen for this volume is a tribute to good librarians, obscure files, creative exploration and luck.

Each of these forgotten photographs was once newsworthy. They are magnificent examples of the art of news photography, capturing some of the world's most beautiful and famous people in ageless glitter and grit. Presented here in never-before-seen detail, the pictures brim with nostalgia, forgotten tales and unmatched charisma and style. They are glimpses of people's lives that together form a slice of Hollywood found. Their realism and surprising intimacy set them apart from any other collection of Hollywood photographs ever published.

The caption information relates only to the picture shown and comes from newspaper files and other biographic sources. The stories are as accurate as the star business allows—given the myths that blur the facts. Sources conflict, and I apologize in advance for any confusion. Dates under the photos are, if possible, publication dates—usually within a few days of the date the photo was taken. Sometimes the dates are unknown or the data differs, in which case I have used historic information to estimate a date ("Circa…").

As the picture detective sorting through the tens of thousands of photographs left in various files, I was regularly awed by the buried images that popped up like time capsules left for a treasure hunt. Two heroes emerge: photo researcher Gayanna Raszkiewicz, from the *Times* photo library, and special collections photo librarian Simon Elliott, from UCLA's Special Collections Library, where most of the negatives are conserved and made available to the public.

Gayanna led me to a yellow cardboard box of lovingly kept contact sheets, which sparked my interest in a book on the lost images of Hollywood lives. Our mutual excitement about the stories the photos told and the impact they still hold carried us through the frustrations of missing, lost and misplaced negatives. Like Indiana Jones and sidekick, we mounted expeditions on our hands and knees through back rooms and dusty files to find the hidden nuggets, the old glass negatives, the stacks of unrecorded negatives, the old folded and dog-eared prints. Gayanna's tidbits of movie trivia always fascinated. She encouraged me when I was bogged down and humored me as I laughed and cried over people and events long past, whose photos still mesmerize by emotions expressed or unexpressed.

At UCLA, Simon was relentless and good-humored as he continued to search negative files that seemed exhausted. Backtracking over unreadable old microfiche records and my plaintive requests to, "please look just one more time," he found the lost and directed me to the unexpected. Some of the most interesting images showed up as unpublished extra negatives tucked in paper envelopes. To find the silver nitrate negatives from the '20s and '30s, we ventured to a chilly vault in Hollywood where we carefully propped open the door with a fire extinguisher to get a little air and some protection lest the volatile early film explode. After we had searched by hand through 36 boxes of useless negatives, Simon's eagle eye spotted a misplaced rogue container that held much of the historic core of the book.

A remarkable group of usually anonymous photojournalists captured the moments of emotion, joy and irony. Since most photographers were male, they helped focus forever the standards of celebrity pictures on the sexy glamour queens. Cameras evolved from bulky models with limited lenses, glass and silver nitrate negatives to large-format safety negatives to the portable 35mm cameras and ranges of films used today. The pioneers of photojournalism lugged their equipment to the courthouse, the police station, the hospital, the cemetery and funeral parlor, to homes, restaurants, family celebrations and crises, through personal sorrows and scandals, and to the premieres and award events that punctuated our city's most famous industry.

Imagic, Inc. in Hollywood created the high-quality prints reproduced in this book. Ever willing to dodge and burn and restore, they pulled everything possible from the brittle and often damaged negatives. Their experts gave depth and importance to the exposures and brought them back to life, paying attention to both editorial and artistic concerns. Becky Stellpflue supervised every print, John Matsunaga printed them and Jack Upston carefully restored them to their original luster. Tim Wild used his digital magic to make whole the often seriously damaged prints for which no negatives could be found.

Mary Peterson's book design rendered both topical focus and aesthetic weight to the photos and their stories. She made the details happen—beautifully. Her interest in, dedication to, and respect for the worth of the project transformed this book into an extraordinary display of sophisticated simplicity. Thank you for the vision, friendship and support. Carla Lazzareschi, Book Development Manager at the *Los Angeles Times*, was willing to chance this endeavor based on a promise and a prayer. Thank you for sticking with it to the end, caring enough to keep pushing for the best, and providing much needed perspective.

I dedicate the book to the photojournalists—their names mostly unknown—who searched for and found these photo opportunities, sometimes in difficult situations and with hostile subjects. They practiced their craft artfully, with little credit and even less respect before their trade was recognized as art. Most of these trailblazers, like their subjects, are now dead. Their work lives. They framed their shots, found the humor and the pathos and the tragedy. Using awkward equipment, they recorded the history of an era in daily pictorial news bites. Decades later, their exposures give us a new vision of Hollywood lives.

Additionally, I want to acknowledge my husband, Daniel McIntosh, and my children, Robby and Douglas McIntosh, who were supportive and patient, if amused, as my conversation turned to ever more obscure intricacies of Hollywood lives (Robby, age 13, saved my computer files more times than I can comfortably admit); Mildred Simpson, the *Times* photo librarian who arranged for the preservation and transfer of the negatives to UCLA at a time when they could easily have been damaged or destroyed, and who was exceptionally helpful and welcoming, as were all others on the staff of the photo library, especially David Cappoli; M. Rosa Gaiarsa, collection services manager of UCLA's Film and Television Archive, who tends the silver nitrate negatives, and Producers and Quality labs, who printed them, both keepers of precious history; Saundra Archer, librarian at the Academy of Motion Picture Arts and Sciences, who helped track down some hidden details; dermatologist-to-the-stars Dr. Mary Lee Amerian, who diagnosed W. C. Fields' skin condition; dentist Dr. Leon D. Katz, who assessed Clark Gable's teeth; Susan Welchman, friend and *National Geographic* editor-colleague, who shared and encouraged my enthusiasm for the photos; Laurie Becklund, Kerry Madden and Mariko Van Kampen, who read and commented on the introductory text; and Bob Van Ee, whom I had not seen since high school, but who was willing to drive to my house on no notice to coax my computer into talking with my printer and scanner.

AMANDA PARSONS is a freelance anthropologist and photojournalist with ten years experience developing book, magazine and research projects for *National Geographic*. Her work is included in the books *Lost Empires*, *Living Tribes*, *Great Rivers of the World* and *Peoples and Places of the Past*, and the magazine feature *The Aztecs*. Her photographs have been published and exhibited internationally.

photo by Ross Elmi, Imagic, Inc.

A listing of reported given names and birth and death dates.

Ameche, Don (Dominic Amici) 1908–1993

Andrews, LaVerne 1915–1967

Andrews, Maxine 1918–1995

Andrews, Patty (Patricia Andrews) 1920

Arnaz, Desi (Desiderio Arnaz y de Acha III) 1917–1997

Astaire, Fred (Frederick Austerlitz) 1899–1987

Bacall, Lauren (Betty or Bette Joan Perske) 1924

Baker, Caroll 1931

Ball, Lucille 1911–1989

Bankhead, Tallulah 1903–1968

Barrymore, John (John Sidney Blythe) 1892–1942

Beatty, Warren (Henry Warren Beaty) 1937

Benny, Jack (Benjamin Kubelsky) 1894–1974

Bergen, Edgar 1903

Blondell, Joan 1909–1979

Bogart, Humphrey 1899–1957

Boone, Debbie or Debby (Deborah Boone) 1956

Boone, Pat (Charles Eugene Boone) 1934

Boyd, William 1895–1972

Brando, Marlon 1924

Bruce, Virginia (Helen Virginia Briggs) 1910–1982

Burke, Billie (Mary William Burke) 1885–1970

Burns, George (Nathan Birnbaum) 1896–1996

Burton, Richard
    (Richard Walter Jenkins, Jr.) 1925–1984

Cagney, James 1899–1986

Chandler, Jeff (Ira Grossel) 1918–1961

Chaplin, Charlie
    (Charles Spencer Chaplin) 1899–1977

Chevalier, Maurice 1888–1972

Coburn, Charles 1877–1961

Cohen, Mickey 1913–1976

Cooper, Gary (Frank James Cooper) 1901–1961

Cooper, Jackie (John Cooper, Jr.) 1921

Costello, Lou (Louis Francis Cristillo) 1906–1959

Crawford, Broderick
    (William Broderick Crawford) 1911–1986

Crawford, Joan (Lucille Fay LeSueur) 1904–1977

Crosby, Bing (Harry Lillis Crosby) 1903–1977

Curtis, Tony (Bernard Schwartz) 1925

Curtiz, Michael 1988–1962

Dahl, Roald 1916–1990

Dandridge, Dorothy 1923–1965

de Havilland, Olivia 1916

De Carlo, Yvonne (Peggy Yvonne Middleton) 1922

Dietrich, Marlene
    (Maria Magdalene Dietrich) 1901–1992

Disney, Walt (Walter Elias Disney) 1901–1966

Durante, Jimmy (James Francis Durante) 1893–1980

Durbin, Deanna (Edna Mae Durbin) 1921

Farmer, Frances 1913–1970

Fields, W.C. (William Claude Dukenfield) 1879–1946

Fisher, Eddie (Edwin Jack Fisher) 1928

Flynn, Errol 1909–1959

Fonda, Henry 1905–1982

Fontaine, Joan (Joan de Beauvoir de Havilland) 1917

Franciosa, Anthony (Anthony Papaleo) 1928

Gable, Clark (William Clark Gable) 1901–1960

Garbo, Greta (Greta Louisa Gustafsson) 1905–1990

Gardner, Ava 1922–1990

Garland, Judy (Frances Gumm) 1922–1969

Garson, Greer 1908–1996

Gilman, Sam 1915–1985

Gleason, Jackie (Herbert John Gleason) 1916–1987

Hargitay, Mickey 1929

Harlow, Jean (Harlean Carpenter) 1911–1937

Haver, June (June Stovenour) 1926

Havoc, June (Ellen Evangeline Hovick) 1916

Hayward, Susan (Edythe Marrener) 1918–1975

Hayworth, Rita
    (Margarita Carmen Cansino) 1918–1987

Henreid, Paul
    (Paul George Julius von Henreid) 1908–1992

Hepburn, Audrey
    (Audrey Hepburn-Ruston) 1929–1993

Hitchcock, Alfred 1899–1980

Holliday, Judy (Judith Tuvim) 1922–1965

Hope, Bob (Leslie Townes Hope) 1903

Hopper, Hedda (Elda Furry) 1890–1966

Hunt, Marsha 1917

Hunter, Tab (Arthur Gelien) 1931

Huston, John 1906–1987

Hutton, Betty (Betty June Thornburg) 1921

Jackson, Michael 1958

Jones, Jennifer (Phyllis Isley) 1919

Kaye, Danny (David Daniel Kaminski) 1913–1987

Keaton, Buster (Joseph Francis Keaton) 1895–1966

Keeler, Ruby (Ethel Hilda Keeler) 1909–1993

Kelly, Grace 1928–1982

Keyes, Evelyn 1919

Khan, Aly 1912–1960

Khrushchev, Nikita 1894–1971

Kitt, Eartha 1928

Lake, Veronica
    (Constance Frances Marie Ockelman) 1919–1973

Lamarr, Hedy (Hedwig Eva Maria Kiesler) 1913

Lancaster, Burt
    (Burton Stephan Lancaster) 1913–1994

Landis, Carole
    (Frances Lillian Mary Ridste) 1919–1948

Leigh, Janet (Jeanette Helen Morrison) 1927

Leigh, Vivien (Vivian Mary Hartley) 1913–1967

Lloyd, Harold 1893–1971

Loder, John (John Muir Lowe) 1898–1988

Lombard, Carole (Jane Alice Peters) 1908–1942

Loren, Sophia (Sofia Sciclone) 1934

Lupino, Ida 1918–1995

Lupino, Stanley 1893–1942

Mac Laine, Shirley (Shirley MacLean Beaty) 1934

Mac Murray, Fred
    (Frederick Martin MacMurray) 1908–1991

Mansfield, Jayne (Vera Jayne Palmer) 1933–1967

March, Fredric (Ernest Frederick Bickel) 1897–1975

Marx, Chico (Leonard Marx) 1886–1961

Marx, Groucho (Julius Henry Marx) 1890 1977

Mayer, Louis B. (Eliezer or Lazar Mayer) 1885–1957

Mayo, Virginia (Virginia Jones) 1920

Mc Daniel, Hattie 1895–1952

Mc Donald, Marie (Cora Marie Frye) 1923–1965

Meredith, Madge 1921

Mineo, Sal (Salvatore Mineo) 1939–1976

Mitchum, Robert 1917–1997

Monroe, Marilyn (Norma Jean Mortenson) 1926–1962

Moreno, Rita (Rosita Dolores Alverio) 1931

Neal, Patricia 1926

Newman, Paul 1925

Niven, David
    (James David Graham Niven) 1909–1985

Novak, Kim (Marilyn Pauline Novak) 1933

O'Brien, Margaret (Angela Maxine O'Brien) 1937

O'Hara, Maureen (Maureen FitzSimons) 1920

Oberon, Merle
    (Estelle Merle O'Brien Thompson) 1911–1979

Olivier, Laurence 1907–1989

Parsons, Louella (Louella Oettinger) 1893–1972

Perreau, Gigi (Ghislaine Perreau-Saussine) 1941

Pickford, Mary (Gladys Smith) 1893–1979

Powell, Dick (Richard Powell) 1904–1963

Powell, William 1892–1984

Power, Tyrone (Tyrone Edmund Power, Jr.) 1913–1958

Presley, Elvis 1935–1977

Quinn, Anthony 1915

Raft, George (George Ranft) 1895–1980

Rathbone, Basil
    (Philip St.John Basil Rathbone) 1892–1967

Reagan, Ronald 1911

Rogers, Roy (Leonard Slye) 1911–1998

Rogers, Will (William Penn Rogers) 1879–1935

Rooney, Mickey (Joe Yule, Jr.) 1920

Russell, Jane (Ernestine Jane Geraldine Russell) 1921

Russell, Gail 1924–1961

Selznick, David Oliver 1902–1965

Shearer, Norma (Edith Norma Shearer) 1900–1983

Sinatra, Frank, Jr. 1944

Sinatra, Frank, Sr. (Francis Albert Sinatra) 1915–1998

Stanwyck, Barbara (Ruby Stevens) 1907–1990

Stewart, Jimmy (James Stewart) 1908–1997

Stompanato, Johnny 1926–1958

Swanson, Gloria

      (Gloria Josephine Swenson) 1897–1983

Taylor, Elizabeth 1932

Taylor, Robert (Spangler Arlington Brugh) 1911–1969

Temple, Shirley 1928

Todd, Michael (Avram Goldenbogen) 1907–1958

Todd, Thelma 1905–1935

Tufts, Sonny (Bowen Charlton Tufts III) 1911–1970

Turner, Lana (Julia Jean Mildred Frances Turner) 1920

Valentino, Rudolph (Rodolfo Guglielmi) 1895–1926

Wagner, Robert 1930

Wald, Jerry (Jerome Irving Wald) 1911–1962

Wallace, Jean (Jean Wallasek) 1923–1990

Wayne, John (Marion Michael Morrison) 1907–1979

Welles, Orson (George Orson Welles) 1915–1985

West, Mae 1892–1980

Wilde, Cornel (Cornelius Louis Wilde) 1915–1989

Wilder, Billy (Samuel Wilder) 1906

Wilding, Michael 1912–1979

Williams, Esther 1923

Winters, Shelley (Shirley Schrift) 1922

Withers, Jane 1926

Wood, Natalie (Natasha Gurdin) 1938–1981

Woodward, Joanne 1930

Wyman, Jane (Sarah Jan Fulks) 1914

Wynn, Ed (Isaiah Edwin Leopold) 1886–1966

Young, Loretta (Gretchen Michaela Young) 1913